The EVOLVE Advantage

Helping You Reach the Outcome You Deserve

Jason Poe

This publication is designed to provide accurate and authoritative information in regard to the subject matter covered. It is sold with the understanding that neither the author nor the publisher is engaged in rendering legal, investment, accounting, health, or other professional services. While the publisher and author have used their best efforts in preparing this book, they make no representations or warranties with respect to the accuracy or completeness of the contents of this book and specifically disclaim any implied warranties of merchantability or fitness for a particular purpose. No warranty may be created or extended by sales representatives or written sales materials. The advice and strategies contained herein may not be suitable for your situation. You should consult with a professional when appropriate. Neither the publisher nor the author shall be liable for any loss of profit or any other commercial or damages, including but not limited to special, incidental, consequential, personal, or other damages.

ISBN: 978-1-968247-78-2 (Digital)

ISBN: 978-1-968247-79-9 (Paperback)

Book Cover by 100Covers

Edited by Ben Heuertz and Bailey Baack

1st Edition 2026

Contents

INTRODUCTION

The Beginning: Why?

"Things work out best for those who make the best of how things work out."

– John Wooden

Have you ever wanted to retire with dignity? Do you have fears about money? Do you want to work with a trusted financial guide to help you develop a financial game plan?

If so, this is the book for you. I am going to share with you a simple and effective process to learn and understand where you are today and the steps that you need to take along the way to reach the outcome that you deserve.

Some of you may just be getting started and for others, you may have been working diligently towards making smart financial decisions for decades. Many of you will have a straightforward situation while others will have a complicated scenario that includes complex details with multiple moving parts to consider. Regardless of where you fall on this spectrum, what I have learned over my 25 years as a financial advisor is that you will have similar fears, emotions and behaviors. It might be simple insecurity or apprehension about making right or wrong decisions. Just because you have been successful financially in another endeavor doesn't mean that you automatically know what the prudent decision may be in any given situation.

Over the years I have dedicated myself to learning how to help my clients find solutions to complicated situations and the resources to do so. Along the way, I have surrounded myself with a competent, dedicated team who I work with every day as well as a group of professionals outside of my practice that we can leverage to assist our holistic approach to improving the financial and emotional well-being of those who allow us to be part of their team. I don't know all the answers, but I know others that do in any given scenario.

But first, I want to share my journey.

Success isn't just about numbers, portfolios, or financial milestones. It's about the journey, the sacrifices, and the growth that comes along the way. Behind every dedicated financial professional is a story of perseverance, late nights, and the unwavering support of those who stand beside them.

When I look back at my career as a financial advisor, I realize it wasn't just about building a business; it was about becoming someone my clients could trust with their futures. But I didn't take this path alone. My wife was there from the beginning, witnessing the long hours, the early mornings, and the moments of doubt. She saw me leave before sunrise and return home just in time for our kids' bedtime. She knew the challenges I faced, the learning curve I had to climb, and the weight of the responsibility I was taking on. Her perspective offers valuable insight into the personal side of this journey, and I'm pleased to share her thoughts:

As the wife of Jason Poe, I was a witness to the beginning of his career as a financial advisor. It has been a rewarding journey to take with him. He decided to go down this path during our first year of marriage. We were both excited and nervous about his future career, but unaware of the amount of time it takes to truly learn how to be a successful financial advisor. By successful, I mean a knowledgeable, mature, conscientious professional who manages the future and many times, the life savings of others. He spent many years going to work by sunrise, eating two meals at his desk, coming in at "bath time" when our children were little, every week, and then going back in on Saturday mornings. It seemed like it would never change, but eventually, it did.

As he started experiencing life's many stages through clients and gaining their trust, his job became a career. One that he loves and is proud of. A career that has given him more satisfaction than most people I know. He says he may not feel like going to the office on occasion, but he never hates his job. He takes his obligations to his clients seriously.

Jason has always had a strong sense of integrity, and with that comes the need to speak frankly. He feels he owes it to his clients in order for them to make the best financial decisions for themselves. This is a point I respect and agree with, although I don't always appreciate it when it focuses on me. It's hard to hear the negative when we want to push ahead but he sees this as his obligation to his clients.

We were right to be nervous at the start of this journey, but also about being excited about all that we would experience along the way. As a new wife, I would pray for his perseverance, that he would maintain a good reputation, and that he would be rewarded for his hard work. My prayers were answered tenfold. I can't imagine another career that would have shaped him into a better man or would be more gratifying. He truly found his calling when he chose financial planning.

In those early years, we were both excited and nervous, unsure of what the future would hold. But over time, through experience and trust, my job became more than a job; it became a career. I've come to love this work, not just for the financial success it has brought but also for the fulfillment of guiding people through some of the most important decisions of their lives. It's a responsibility I don't take lightly and has shaped me in ways I never expected.

How did I get here?

I had already built a business that was doing well, but I did not know how to scale it, so I decided to take on a new career. I had a couple of friends in the industry, one of whom was a roommate working as a traditional stockbroker, and he was doing well. He was a college friend, and I felt like if he could do it, then I could as well, and that's how I got started.

I started in the financial services industry in late 1999. I was a career changer and looking to do something different, but my timing could have been better. What I didn't know at the time was that the tech bubble was about to burst. The tech bubble was created as the internet came into common use and internet-based companies became popular investments. There was a ton of speculative investing coupled with a lack of due diligence starting in the mid 1990's culminating with the NASDAQ peaking in March 2020. What followed was a drop of over 50%, which lead to the recession of 2001. By October of 2002 the NASDAQ had fallen over 70% from its previous high. Many of these tech companies went out of business or suffered significantly and we saw many formerly highly compensated employees now out of work.

I didn't realize it at the time, but getting started during such a rough period with the economy, markets and watching people lose their jobs was an important learning experience. It didn't feel like it at the time, but seeing the damage and heartache inflicted upon the clients of many of my advisor peers really caught my attention. It feels strange to say it now, but thankfully I didn't have many clients since I was just getting started, so to a certain degree I avoided watching my clients suffer during a difficult time.

I got my start with a company that underwrote some small American Stock Exchange (AMEX) deals and private placements.

They had a broker side and an investment banking side. I started on the broker side, and after about six months, I was moved to the banking side and was there for another six months. Over my time there, I realized that the company wasn't the right fit for me, but I enjoyed the industry.

So, I moved to a company that did financial planning rather than pitching stocks and mutual funds, leaving my role as a more traditional stockbroker to become a financial planner. And that was a wonderful experience for me. That's where I learned the industry's nuts and bolts and I think of my time there as the official start of my career as a financial planner.

After about seven years, I had the opportunity to join Southwestern Investment Group located in Nashville, Tennessee. (now SageSpring Wealth Advisors)

Southwestern Investment Group was started and led by Jeff Dobyns. As the leader, Jeff had developed a professional relationship with Dave Ramsey who lived in the area. He is the author of Financial Peace fame, among other accomplishments including Financial Peace University. The firm, Southwestern Investment Group, was an Endorsed Local Provider (ELP) for Dave, where Dave fans could go online and put in their contact information, and an Endorsed Local Provider would reach out to them to see how they could help with financial planning, investments and insurance.

As I recall, Dave was becoming more popular nationwide and was expanding into different markets, one of which was the Dallas, Texas area, where I was living. As I understand it, he was pleased with the service that the team in Nashville was providing as ELPs locally and essentially said, "Hey, do you guys want to move into the Dallas market?" The answer was yes, but no one raised their hand to move to Dallas. Lucky me!

A friend recommended me as a local financial advisor that might be a good fit for the team. I met with the leadership of Southwestern Investment Group, and I was impressed. The opportunity looked good on paper, as the saying goes, but I had built up a ton of goodwill with the company I was associated with then. However, I took a leap of faith, said yes, and opened the first office for Southwestern Investment Group outside of Nashville, in Frisco, Texas. It is undoubtedly the best career decision I have ever made, and I am so grateful that I was given the opportunity. That was in late 2006, and it continues to benefit me, my family, my business, and the teammates I am fortunate to have working alongside me.

Much like my start in the industry just before the tech bubble popped, my timing could have been more opportune. Unknown at that time, but just around the corner was the Great Recession, which was the worst recession since the Great Depression in 1930.

From late 2007 through early 2009 the US economy and markets took a beating. As a result of the Great Recession, the United States alone lost more than 8.7 million jobs, according to the U.S. Bureau of Labor Statistics, doubling the unemployment rate. Further, U.S. households lost roughly $19 trillion in net worth as the stock market plunged, according to the U.S. Department of the Treasury. The Great Recession's official end date was June 2009.

Once again, witnessing such a difficult time early in my career has proven to be beneficial. The number of clients that I had was materially higher than when the dot.com bubble burst, but I do believe that some of the lessons that I had learned then benefited my clients.

As the first financial advisor in Frisco for the Southwestern Investment Group, most of my clients were a result of my association with the Dave Ramsey Show as an Endorsed Local Provider (ELP). That is when my career really began to take off.

Breaking into the industry as a financial advisor was exceedingly difficult, much more so than I ever anticipated. While I was trying to get going, I spent every penny I had and then some, quickly going into debt trying to get over the hump. There were days when I did not know if I would make it, and I mentally quit many times driving home from the office. Thankfully, I always changed my mind by morning and made the hour commute to the office to fight another day.

I continued to work hard, and with a little good luck was able to slowly establish a successful financial planning practice. I credit my wife, Melissa, for a large part of my success. She had a respectable job with a steady income, which was huge financially for our family. Also, she believed in the dream of building a business where I could have a meaningful impact on people's lives. Most importantly, she gave me the emotional support that I needed. As I slowly built my business, I could put down the shovel, so to speak, and was finally no longer creating more debt.

What I mean by getting over the hump is that I was no longer going further in debt, but I was not really getting out either. I wasn't doing what I call backfilling, meaning that I couldn't pay down my debt materially. So, that kept me in a state of sort of treading water, not getting out of debt, but not creating more. Thankfully, over time, I was able to pay off everything, excluding my house, and was finally back to a level playing field

During our struggle, Melissa and I added to our family, eventually having three kids: one daughter and two boys. My wife and kids have given me a tremendous amount of joy and continue to do so, but kids are not inexpensive. So, as things improved for my business and income, I had what I call a competition for my resources.

That competition can broadly be defined as now and in the future. The "now" includes things like building and maintaining an emergency fund, funding activities that my children were involved with, such as dancing for my daughter and multiple sports for both of my boys. Another "now" was family vacations, which were important to us, and we learned to have them in a budget-friendly fashion, which allowed us to create some great memories.

We did a lot of summer trips in the mountains to escape the summer heat in Texas, which included tons of day hikes with a picturesque view for our inexpensive picnic lunch. Texas has a coastline, but it isn't anywhere near the Dallas area where we live. However, it is close enough to drive, which makes it more economical. Admittedly, there are more beautiful beaches than in Texas, but it doesn't cost anything to have beach access, which made them another great place for a fun time and more cheap picnic lunches. These are just a couple of examples, but my point is that you can do some fun things with your family, make some fond memories and not break the bank.

Essentially, what I am trying to communicate is that you want to make smart financial decisions, but having a life and enjoying your family is important. Sitting at home watching the grass grow and eating ketchup sandwiches might be necessary sometimes, but you can have a little fun without going overboard.

In the "later" category, things such as saving for college and retirement come into play. When I say "later," I don't mean waiting until later to get started. My point is that you will probably not retire until sometime in the future, but you will wake up one day and the future will be now, so start early. As mentioned, I spent everything I had, including draining my retirement accounts, to start my business. However, once I was out of debt and had my emergency fund in place, I immediately started saving again for retirement. Was I saving as much as I would have liked to…no! But it is critically important that you get started with even a small amount ASAP; the time value of money is a real thing. As Einstein reportedly said, *"Interest is the eighth wonder of the world."*

CHAPTER ONE

The Education Gap

"How long are you going to wait before you demand the best for yourself?"

– Epictetus

There are many rules of thumb when it comes to saving and investing toward your goals, but these are 5 of my favorites that I believe are useful for almost anyone:

1. **The 10% Rule**: If you save 10% of your earnings throughout your working life and achieve reasonable investment performance, you're likely to retire into a lifestyle similar to what you have become accustomed to.

2. **Start Early and Be Consistent:** The earlier you start saving, the more time your money has to grow. Consistency is key, whenever possible set up automatic savings to make it effortless.

3. **Increase Savings as Income Grows**: Try to boost your savings rate as your career advances and income increases. This accelerates your wealth accumulation.

4. **Protect Your Savings**: While savings are crucial, it's also important to have safeguards like health insurance, life insurance, and disability coverage to protect against unforeseen circumstances that could derail your financial plans.

5. **The Lifetime of Taxes**: Generally, you can't completely avoid paying taxes, but there are things that you can do to minimize them both now and in the future. By holding onto more of your money and in some instances, controlling when you must pay taxes, you naturally keep more of your money. Ideally, these tax savings are invested and growing over time.

At its most basic level, money doesn't come with an instruction manual. We could criticize our educational system or society for the lack of fundamental financial education, but the fact remains that this knowledge is often overlooked. Financial matters are rarely discussed in casual settings, perhaps due to their perceived taboo or fear of showboating.

Money is inherently intimate; it is very personal and means different things to different people. Also, I have found that there are some generational trends that are almost hard-wired for some people. One example is that children of the Great Depression have a true fear that they can lose everything overnight, which can cause them to be overly conservative and cautious with their financial decisions. It's tied to self-worth and can evoke strong emotions and judgments. In many ways, discussing finances is as personal as discussing health with a doctor. After one's health, financial well-being is generally one of the more important personal considerations. Yet, it's rarely discussed openly, causing many of us to get a late start on our financial journey.

A startling statistic highlights the importance of this issue: approximately half of Americans have no retirement savings whatsoever, relying solely on Social Security. While Social

Security is a valuable benefit, it's insufficient to provide a comfortable retirement for most of us. Many retirees find that Social Security benefits struggle to keep pace with inflation, and increases in payments are often offset by rises in Medicare costs. That's why investing earlier and smarter is paramount.

Time can be your ally or your adversary. Having more of a financial runway is always preferable, but our consumerist and materialistic culture presents a challenge to financial education and healthy financial habits. Marketing has been perfected to convince us that we deserve immediate gratification. Popular media often portrays lifestyles that require substantial wealth, which can be misleading.

This is why it's essential to remember that comparison is the thief of joy. We must be cautious about setting goals and comparing ourselves to others based on others' apparent success or lifestyle. Some may have different objectives, started earlier, or might not be saving at all, potentially harming their long-term financial health. Everyone has different goals they are trying to achieve. Some people may want to travel the world during retirement, while others want to stay closer to home and spend time with their grandchildren; everyone is different.

My goal is to help people understand their financial truth and what that means for them and their situation. The good news is that it's not overly complicated; it's about developing good habits. By creating and maintaining these habits, most people can reach their financial goals. Two basic concepts to focus on are avoiding common mistakes and implementing the right strategies. When combined, these simple approaches can significantly improve one's financial situation.

The reality is that some of you are just getting started and need assistance identifying good habits to follow. For others, you have traveled further down the road and have already done a great job of planning and saving for the goals that are important to you. The question for someone in either scenario is this: Are you sure that you are doing everything that you should and can be doing, and are you on track to reach your goals?

At its essence, my job is about preventing people from making bad decisions (aka dumb stuff) and helping them make good decisions (aka smart stuff) with their money. While that may not sound particularly glamorous, it's the foundation of sound financial planning. Therefore, I aim to present this information in the clearest way possible, making it easy for anyone to understand and apply it to their lives, regardless of whether you are just getting started or have already built a significant nest egg.

While it's possible for individuals to manage their own finances successfully, there are several reasons why many choose to work with a financial advisor.

For most people, financial planning isn't a passion or hobby. Even if you're capable of managing your finances, it may not be how you want to spend your free time. It's like home repairs–sure, you may be handy and can probably repair your air conditioner yourself if it quits on you, but it might take a 3-day weekend and 10 trips to Home Depot. Meanwhile, a professional might be able to diagnose the issue quickly and have the part needed in their service truck, which is way more efficient.

Money is inherently emotional, and the impact of financial decisions increases with the amount involved. Losing 10% on a $10,000 investment feels different than losing 10% on a

$1,000,000 investment, even though the percentage is the same. This emotional component can cloud judgment and interfere with rational decision-making. I believe that it is important to think through and make important financial decisions when there are no ripples on the water, so that when you have a financial storm, you are not making decisions while you are fighting rough seas and bailing water to stay afloat. A financial advisor provides an objective perspective, helping to provide accountability for financial choices.

Much like a personal trainer at the gym, a financial advisor serves as an accountability partner. They ensure you're consistently working towards your financial goals, even when motivation wanes. Also, it's like routinely seeing your doctor and following their advice to help you prevent a problem before it happens - preventative medicine. This consistency is necessary for long-term financial success. Much like sparse workouts, sparse attention to finances is better than nothing, but unlikely to yield optimal results.

A financial advisor offers expert knowledge and, perhaps more importantly, serves as a sounding board for ideas. They can provide informed opinions on financial decisions, offer alternative perspectives, or direct you to other experts when needed. This collaborative approach helps in making more informed and well-rounded financial decisions. I find that sometimes I need to pull my clients back from the water's edge, and at other times, encourage them to get in the water.

A good financial advisor earns trust over time and provides honest, sometimes difficult feedback. They should have the strength of character to tell you when an idea or action isn't in your best interest, rather than simply agreeing with everything you suggest. This honesty helps lead to long-term financial success.

While advisors sometimes need to deliver unwelcome news or challenge a client's thinking, the most effective approach is often to guide clients to realize certain truths on their own. When clients reach conclusions on their own, I have found that they're more likely to take ownership of the decision and follow through. By being another set of eyes and talking through ideas and issues that someone may be dealing with at any given time, that exercise can lead a client to the appropriate decision or plan of action on their own.

A financial advisor's role goes beyond number-crunching. They serve as a guide, a voice of reason, and a partner in your financial journey, helping you navigate the complex and often emotional world of personal finance. Much like someone who intends to climb Mount Everest, you need a guide or sherpa to show you the way. They can help you avoid known pitfalls, take the best route for success, know when and where to shelter from a storm, and let you know if making the summit is too dangerous on a given day. Most importantly, they work to help you complete the trip and safely make it back to base camp.

An interesting part of my role involves asking clients to explain their financial reasoning when I sense that they are about to make a questionable decision. Often, as they talk through their ideas, they realize on their own when something doesn't make sense. This self-realization is far more impactful than if I were to simply tell them what to do.

Three broad-based rules that I preach:

1. **Debt management:** Distinguishing between good debt (like a reasonable mortgage) and bad debt (credit cards, personal loans, 401K loans) and creating strategies to eliminate the latter.
2. **Emergency saving/Cash reserve:** Ensuring clients have funds set aside for unexpected events or "rainy days." There are always bumps in the road or something waiting around the corner it seems.
3. **Utilizing appropriate savings vehicles:** Helping clients choose the right tools to work toward short-term and long-term financial goals. Using a shovel when you need a hammer isn't ideal.

The first rule of "holes" is to put down the shovel. If you find yourself in a financial hole, stop digging. It's about backfilling and establishing a stable foundation before moving forward. Sometimes, this means addressing immediate concerns before focusing on long-term planning and investments.

A great example of good financial habits came early in my career; I had the opportunity to work with a young nurse who exemplified the power of consistent saving and good financial habits. She had just graduated from nursing school as an LVN (Licensed Vocational Nurse) when her father, a client, sent her to me for financial advice. Her approach was ideal–she came in ready to follow whatever guidance I offered regarding her money management.

We started with a modest savings plan, likely around $50 to $100 per month. The key was consistency–she developed the habit of saving regularly without thinking about it. I'm a strong advocate for what I call "dummy-proofing" finances, and one such example is where money is automatically transferred to savings and retirement accounts on a set schedule.

As her career progressed, so did her savings. She became an RN (Registered Nurse), and over time a Physician's Assistant, increasing her contributions as her income grew. She maintained her emergency fund, consistently saved into retirement accounts, and resisted the temptation to withdraw funds for non-essential purposes.

Over the next ten to twelve years, starting from a relatively modest salary of maybe $40,000 annually, increasing to around $100,000 or so, she managed to accumulate approximately $100,000 in investments as I remember it. This achievement wasn't due to picking the best investments or having an extraordinarily high income. It was the result of consistent, early, and frequent saving, coupled with the discipline to let the money grow undisturbed.

This example demonstrates how beneficial good habits are and how powerful starting your financial planning early can be. The sooner you start, the more opportunity you have to make small adjustments to reach your goals. When people wait longer to start planning, any necessary changes can be more significant and challenging to implement. Hence, start when you have a longer runway to gain the necessary speed to take off and fly.

Reaching your desired financial destination doesn't have to be complicated. With the right tools and guidance, it is straightforward. That's why I created a process called The EVOLVE Advantage, a simple, accessible framework to help anyone feel more confident about their financial future. It's all about making informed decisions, avoiding common mistakes, and staying on track toward your goals. By following this process and working with a trusted advisor, you can build a strong foundation that supports your life and provides security for you and your loved ones. EVOLVE stands for Establish, Visualize, Orient, Learn, Vote, and Evaluate–a step-by-step approach to defining your financial path, setting clear goals, adjusting as needed, and making decisions that align with what really matters to you. In each chapter, we will cover a new step of the process and dive into lessons I have picked up along the way.

Generally, building wealth isn't about complex strategies or getting lucky with hot investments. It's about establishing good habits, being consistent, and allowing time and compound interest to work in your favor. The key is to start now, save regularly, and stay on the course. You start by taking the first step and then putting one foot in front of the other.

Making small sacrifices, like occasionally staying in instead of going out, can make a significant difference over time. While extreme frugality isn't enjoyable for most people, sometimes financial restraint is necessary to achieve long-term goals. To paraphrase Dave Ramsey, "If you will live like no one else now, later you can live like no one else," which emphasizes the importance of making sacrifices to achieve future financial success and everything that comes with it.

We can bridge the gap between financial uncertainty and financial security by addressing the financial education gap, overcoming societal challenges, seeking professional guidance when needed, and implementing sound, consistent financial habits

CHAPTER TWO

Behavior, Emotion, and Coordination

"Investing success doesn't correlate with IQ after you're above a score of 25. Once you have ordinary intelligence, then what you need is the temperament to control urges that get others into trouble."

– Warren Buffett

Before beginning our journey through the EVOLVE Advantage process, I want to spend what will take you 10 minutes to read on behaviors or to say it another way, emotions. I will make references to behaviors throughout sharing this process, how it works, and how I have seen it apply in the real world. That said, this is an important component that deserves attention.

There are numerous cognitive behaviors that I could share with you, but these ten examples are what I would put in the common category based on my experience.

Confirmation Bias: The tendency to search for, interpret, and remember information in a way that confirms one's preexisting beliefs, while giving less consideration to alternative possibilities.

Example: a gardener who only waters the plants they believe will thrive and ignores the others. This selective attention can lead to poor decisions, as the gardener overlooks crucial signs that some plants (in our case investments) may need more care.

Loss Aversion: People prefer to avoid losses rather than receiving equivalent gains. It implies that the pain of losing is more impactful than the pleasure of gaining.

Example: the idea that you are more upset about losing a $100 bill than you are happy about finding one. This emotional response often leads investors to hold onto losing stocks too long or sell winning stocks too early, driven by the fear of loss rather than the potential for gain.

Hindsight Bias: One sees events as having been predictable after they have already occurred. This leads people to believe that they "knew it all along" when, in fact, they did not.

Example: a gambler who claims they knew a particular team would win the championship after the game is over, despite having doubts before the match. This bias can lead investors to overestimate their ability to predict market movements.

Availability Heuristic: A shortcut that relies on immediate examples that come to a person's mind when evaluating something.

Example: choosing a restaurant based on the most recent advertisements you have seen, rather than considering all available options. This can lead to poor investment decisions, as individuals may overestimate the importance of market headlines.

Anchoring Bias: The tendency to rely too heavily on the first piece of information encountered (the "anchor") when making decisions.

Example: a ship dropping anchor in a harbor; the ship may drift with the current, but it will only move within the limits set by the anchor's chain. Similarly, when making financial decisions, individuals often rely heavily on an initial piece of information, which can restrict their ability to adjust their judgments when new data is available.

Overconfidence Bias: This bias is characterized by an individual's excessive confidence in their own answers, judgments, or abilities.

Example: someone who believes they are an exceptional driver, so they ignore road signs and traffic rules leading to an accident. Just as the driver overestimates their skills, investors may overestimate their abilities, resulting in risky financial choices.

Framing Effect: The way information is presented can significantly affect decisions and judgments.

Example: having a choice between two investment options presented differently: one option states, *"You have a 70% chance of making a profit,"* while the other says, *"You have a 30% chance of losing money."* Despite both statements conveying the same risk, people are more likely to choose the first option due to its positive framing.

Recency Bias: The tendency to give greater importance to the most recent information, which can distort decision-making and perceptions of trends.

Example: the diehard Dallas Cowboys fan who only remembers the last few games their team played and won, believing that their recent performance will continue. This can lead investors to make poor decisions, such as buying stocks after a recent surge or selling during a downturn, rather than considering the overall historical performance.

Herd Mentality Bias: The tendency for individuals to adopt the behaviors, beliefs, or opinions of a larger group.

Example: when fall and winter begin to set in, flocks of birds fly south in unison; when one bird changes direction, the rest follow without questioning why. This behavior can lead to significant market movements, such as bubbles or crashes, as investors mimic each other's actions.

Endowment Effect: A bias where people assign more value to things they own, leading to an irrational reluctance to trade or sell those items.

Example: someone who buys their company stock at $50. Even if the market value drops to $30, they may refuse to sell it, believing it is worth more simply because they are employed there, rather than recognizing the current market value.

Financial decision-making is often assumed to be a rational process guided by logical assessments of risk and reward. However, research in behavioral finance has consistently demonstrated that cognitive biases play a crucial role in shaping investment behavior and personal financial choices. Biases can lead to suboptimal decisions. Understanding the psychological underpinnings of financial behavior is essential to mitigate risks associated with irrational decision-making.

So how do we work with our clients towards reducing behaviors and bias that we all have to some degree or another?

There are two approaches to decision-making as outlined by Daniel Kahneman in his book *Thinking Fast and Slow*:

- **Reflexive (System 1)** – Going with your gut, which is effortless, automatic and, in fact, is our default option

- **Reflective (System 2)** – Logical and methodical, but requires effort to engage in actively

When we use reflexive decision-making, we become more prone to deceptive biases and emotional and social influences. Therefore, it is best to establish logical decision-making processes that can help protect you from such errors.

I cannot stress enough how people's behaviors, emotions, and personal experiences influence their financial decisions and attitudes towards wealth. Understanding money is not just about math and formulas, but also about our behavior and the complex relationship we have with our finances. I believe that success with money is more about behavior than being an expert on knowing what to do at any given time.

By implementing The EVOLVE Advantage with our clients, we focus on the process rather than the outcome. Focusing on the process will lead to better decisions because the process helps you engage in reflective decision-making.

Fragmented Financial Planning

In medicine, there's a term called fragmented care. It happens when a patient sees multiple providers who don't coordinate. One doctor prescribes a medication, another unrelated physician orders a duplicate test, who in turn prescribes a new, different medication. The new medication might work at cross purposes with the other original medication or possibly create a new issue which then must be addressed, possibly compounding the initial medical issue that the patient was working on to address. The result often leads to confusion, higher costs, and worse outcomes.

Personal finance suffers from the same problem. It's called fragmented financial planning. What it looks like:

- An investment advisor builds a portfolio without asking about future taxes.
- A CPA minimizes this year's tax bill but ignores the long-term impact of taxes in retirement.
- An insurance agent sells life insurance coverage without understanding how it affects estate and tax planning already in place.
- An attorney drafts a will, unaware that there is life insurance coverage in place that is intended to be used towards estate taxes or to equalize the asset transfer between beneficiaries.
- An investment advisor isn't aware that an attorney created a family trust and that account registrations and beneficiaries need to be updated.

Each professional may do their job well in isolation, but the overall plan doesn't hold together. Advisors often work in silos, focusing only on their individual specialty rather than coordinating with other professionals. Major life changes such as marriage, children, inheritance, job transitions, or retirement can quickly render a once-sound plan outdated. And many people fall into tunnel vision, seeking help for a single issue like taxes, investments, or insurance without recognizing how deeply interconnected those areas truly are.

The consequences of fragmentation can be significant. It often leads to higher costs through redundant strategies, unnecessary fees, or missed tax savings. It can also create gaps in coverage, leaving critical risks either unaccounted for or poorly managed. Families may miss opportunities that only work when strategies are coordinated across multiple disciplines. And instead of feeling confident, clients juggling conflicting advice from different professionals frequently experience more confusion and stress.

Coordinated financial planning creates a multiplier effect. Like a family that communicates openly, a financial team that works together produces more than the sum of its parts. One plus one can equal three. Integration ensures that strategies don't collide but reinforce one another.

I worked with a couple who embodied this issue. They had a stockbroker managing investments, a CPA handling taxes, and an attorney who drafted their Wills years earlier. Each professional was competent, but none spoke to the others. The result was a patchwork plan that left major tax inefficiencies and outdated estate documents. When we finally pulled the pieces together, aligning investments with tax strategy, updating legal documents, and reviewing insurance, they were shocked by how much smoother, simpler, and more secure their financial life became.

The EVOLVE Advantage was built to counter this problem. By following a structured process and insisting on integration, it ensures that every financial decision fits into the bigger picture.

Bridging these gaps doesn't mean having all the answers on day one. You just have to take deliberate steps, like adopting sound rules of thumb, seeking guidance when needed, and demanding integration instead of fragmentation. The education gap is closed through learning. The guidance gap is closed through partnership. The integration gap is closed through coordination. Together, these bridges create a financial life that is technically sound and emotionally steady.

There are more "unknowns" in life than we can count and manage effectively. However, if we can identify and incorporate some of the more obvious things such as emotion, behavior and coordination we can provide a more solid foundation towards implementing and successfully executing a comprehensive financial plan. The different steps in The EVOLVE Advantage process assist both the financial advisor and the client to address and revisit these important, but less obvious "unknowns."

CHAPTER THREE

Establish Your Situation:

Where Are You Now?

"Start from wherever you are and with whatever you've got."

– Jim Rohn

The first 'E' in EVOLVE stands for **Establish**, which is about determining your current financial situation, where you are today. When planning a journey, you need to know your starting point before you can chart a course to your destination.

The Establish phase is typically a little bit boring and can be cumbersome. It is gathering documents that are often spread out in many different places that require a username and password that you can't find and that's if you even know the web address for what it is that you are trying to locate. In a couple's scenario, you may be organized, but your spouse may not be and that can create an extra hurdle to make the process even more difficult.

Some of the common concerns or reasons for not getting started that I hear are: You feel like it's too late, and you've missed your chance to build real financial security. You're worried that diving into this will cause friction at home—that your spouse isn't on board or that money conversations will lead to arguments. I don't have time for this, between work, kids, and everything else, how would I even fit it in? My plate is full currently, and I already feel overwhelmed. Why would I add additional stress? But let's be honest, sometimes it's easier to focus on more immediate priorities than to sit down and gather financial documents.

And then, of course, there's the fear that looking at your financial reality will reveal things you don't want to see. What if it's bad? What if I've made mistakes? What if I'm too far behind to catch up?

To hear the opposite is also common, I've got a pile of money and if I can't live on that I have a problem. I have always been a good saver; I am ahead of most people I know, and I feel sure that I will be fine.

These are real thoughts. Real concerns. And they keep people stuck. But this doesn't make the problems go away, it only makes them harder to solve later should you learn that you are not on track to accomplish what is important to you. Taking the first step is never easy, but it's necessary.

In financial terms, establishing your situation involves answering questions such as:

- Do you have a debt that needs to be addressed?
- Do you have an emergency fund?
- If you have children, do you have life insurance to protect them financially?
- Have you started saving? If so, where and how much?
- Do you have any retirement accounts that need to be considered?
- Is your net worth or investible assets highly concentrated in a particular sector or company?

- Do you have a significant tax issue that you need to be aware of and planning to address?
- Are there things that you can be doing right now that would reduce your taxes today?
- Are you a business owner and potentially subject to litigation or creditors that could wipe out your business?

This step requires honesty and thoroughness. While most of this information is readily available, gathering everything may take some effort, especially details about old accounts or investments. That's why so many people put it off. However, when you take the time to do this, it creates a clear picture of where you stand financially and is an inventory of where you are today.

The "Establish" phase helps determine whether you need to focus on "putting down the shovel" and filling in financial holes, or if you have a solid foundation and can immediately start working towards more exciting goals like growing your investments.

I can promise you that no one drives around a neighborhood looking at homes to potentially purchase and gets excited about the foundation. It's simply not very sexy or exciting. But what are you thinking? It is something closer to wow, what a beautiful house, I can see us living there. But the foundation is one of the most, if not the most important part of a house. You can build an impressive structure, but if the foundation fails it all comes falling down. Focusing on your financial foundation may not get you especially excited, but it is the base of everything that you will build on.

Establishing your current financial situation is the essential first step in any financial journey. It provides the foundation for all other financial decisions and strategies.

To establish someone's financial reality, we start by providing a questionnaire that is designed to capture all your financial "stuff," and then some along with a list of documents that we need to gather and review.

I've seen it time and time again, people struggle to take this first step because of deeply ingrained beliefs, fears, and excuses:

- *"I'm too busy."* People often feel too busy with work and family commitments to focus on financial planning.
- *"I'll do it later."* There's a tendency to believe planning for the future can wait until later.
- *"What if it's bad?"* Some avoid financial planning because they're afraid of discovering unfavorable information about their financial situation.
- *"It takes too much effort."* Gathering financial information, such as details from old employer accounts or current benefits, can seem daunting.
- *"I have more important things to focus on right now."* It's often easier to choose immediate gratification, like watching a movie or going out, over financial planning.

Unfortunately, it often takes a major life event to prompt people to seek professional financial advice. Common catalysts include:

- Loss of a loved one

- Job loss
- Pressure from a spouse
- Witnessing others' financial struggles
- Approaching life milestones (e.g., children getting closer to college, nearing retirement age)

These events can serve as wake-up calls, making people realize the importance of financial planning and preparation, and the potential consequences of inaction.

But why wait for a crisis? Why not start now, when you are in a position of control versus outside events driving your decisions not at the time of your choosing.

Ideally, financial planning should begin as soon as you enter adulthood and start your professional life. Taking basic financial steps early can make a significant difference even if you're unsure of your long-term goals. Here's why:

1. **Start early:** Beginning to save and make smart financial decisions in your early 20s can provide more flexibility later when you have competing financial priorities, such as raising children, starting a business or perhaps caring for elderly parents.

2. **Utilizing employer benefits:** Understanding and maximizing your employer's benefits package can provide crucial protection and savings opportunities in a cost-efficient manner.

3. **Basic protections:** Securing essential protections such as health, life, and long-term disability insurance.

4. **Basic estate planning documents (Will, power of attorney, medical power of attorney and medical directives):** These are incredibly important, even if you don't have substantial assets yet.

5. **Good financial habits:** Start contributing at least 10% to a 401(k) and take advantage of employer matching when it is available (literally free money!).

6. **Flexibility for the unexpected:** Having a solid financial foundation allows you to adjust to both positive and negative life changes more easily.

When looking at the above reasons to start early, one really stands out as it relates to investing: compounding. Assuming a hypothetical 7% annualized rate of return on an investment, you double your money about every 10 years. Or even better, with a hypothetical 10% annualized rate of return on an investment, you double your money roughly every 7 years. The more of these hypothetical 7- or 10-year periods you have over time means that the "doubling" gets crazy. The same math that turns $1,000 into $2,000 also would turn $1,000,000 into $2,000,000. Let compounding be your friend.

Thinking about compounding in the inverse can be helpful. For example, to reach $1,000,000 by the age of 65 with an 8% annualized rate of return, a 25-year-old would have to invest $530 a month or $6,360 per year. For a 35-year-old to reach the same goal they would have to invest $649 per month totaling $7,788 a year. Finally, a 45-year-old would have to invest $1,748 each month or $20,976 each year to accomplish the same goal.

	Monthly Investment	Annual Investment
Starting Age of 25	$530	$6,360
Starting Age of 35	$649	$7,788
Starting Age of 45	$1,748	$20,976

Your financial plan can be adjusted accordingly as your life and career evolve. Don't wait for a crisis or major life event to start thinking about your financial future. Don't let fear, procrastination, or the feeling of being overwhelmed hold you back.

Many people miss out on significant opportunities by waiting too long to take that first step. They thought they had time. They thought they'd figure it out later. But later came, and they wished they had started sooner.

Even if you feel you don't have much to plan for yet, starting early with basic steps can set you on the right path and make future financial decisions easier. No matter where you are today, get started. A saying that I like about when to plant a tree helps make my point – the best time to have planted a tree was 25 years ago, the next best time is to plant it today.

To conclude this phase of the process, let's look at an example from a client. Early in my career I was just getting started with a couple that I hoped would become a client. While gathering information it became shockingly clear that this couple had a life insurance need that wasn't being covered. So, before we even completed this step, I helped this family get a cheap term life insurance policy which is a cost-efficient way to cover the risk of unexpected death. Together, we worked our way through The EVOLVE Advantage process which they found valuable, and they eventually became clients.

Unfortunately, Mr. Client passed away unexpectedly two or three years later. Through his employer, he did have a 401K, and a robust employer sponsored pension along with a small group life insurance contract. However, the term policy that they had taken out outside of his employer plan made a material difference. It allowed his wife, who was a stay-at-home mother, to grieve without worrying about money. Thankfully, she was able to continue to be a homemaker until their children graduated from high school. Once the kids were out of the house she did enter the workforce; however, she had not worked outside the home in close to 20 years.

She was essentially starting as an entry level employee and was being compensated as such. The good news is that the proceeds from life insurance along with the other benefits through her husband's employer allowed her to live comfortably in a lifestyle that she was accustomed to living.

CHAPTER FOUR

Visualize Your Future:

Where Do You Want to Go?

"They did not know it was impossible, so they did it."

– Mark Twain

After establishing your current financial situation, the second step in The EVOLVE Advantage process is to **Visualize** your financial future. This stage involves setting goals and dreaming about what you want your future to look like.

Based on my twenty-five years of experience, most people become interested in their finances and financial planning around the age of 45-50. This is typically when their financial resources have increased, and they start to feel that they can begin looking towards the future, as their children become more independent.

The visualization step is about imagining where you want to go financially. It's a bit like daydreaming about your ideal future. This is an exciting step in the process, when you begin to mentally build that house on your boring, but strong foundation. Common themes that emerge during this process include:

How long might you want to work? Some clients want to work as long as possible, while others can't wait to retire. Both perspectives require planning.

- What is important as it relates to your values or spirituality?
- Maybe it's building memories for you and a spouse, your children and potentially grandkids?
- Lifestyle goals: These can include traveling, engaging in charitable work, or pursuing hobbies like golfing, fishing, or gardening.
- Family considerations: Many clients express a desire to live near their children and grandchildren in retirement.
- Location preferences: Some clients dream of a lake house, mountain retreat, or beach home.

Many people avoid thinking too far ahead because the future feels uncertain. But here's the truth: the earlier you start thinking about it, the more control you have over shaping it.

It's important to note that this vision doesn't need to be perfect or extremely detailed. The goal is to get headed in the right direction, understanding that plans may change over time. Often, just thinking about what your future will look like in 10 years is a good way to get the process started. Putting more time aside for visualization provides more flexibility to modify your goals as you progress through life stages.

During the visualization process, people often experience a range of emotions and concerns:

- **Uncertainty:** Many people struggle to articulate what they want their future to look like. It's common to hear "I don't know" in response to questions about future goals.

- **Perfectionism:** Some individuals try to be too precise in their vision, wanting to plan every detail. Specific steps are important, but it's important to remember that flexibility is key, as circumstances will likely change.
- **Fear of disappointment:** Some individuals worry that their vision might be unrealistic, and they're afraid of receiving bad news later in the process.
- **Resistance to change:** There's often concern about having to make immediate lifestyle changes to achieve future goals.
- **Difficulty with long-term thinking:** For some, making even broad decisions about the future is challenging.

Visualization is also a team effort. Although you and your partner may have different goals for the future, this allows you to get on the same page and create a vision for the future that you both are motivated to achieve.

When done right, you are truly dreaming about your ideal future. This is unique to you and whatever your reasoning, we want to paint a picture of this dream and create a path to get you there.

My role is to guide people through this process, helping them articulate their vision while maintaining realistic expectations. The visualization step is crucial in setting the direction for the financial planning process, even if the specifics change over time.

The outcomes vary dramatically when I assess a client's current situation and future goals. In some cases, I deliver good news: they could retire sooner or accomplish more in retirement than anticipated. However, in other instances, I have to deliver challenging news, like the harsh reality that they overextended themselves financially. In extreme cases, I have had to advise families to consider selling their homes–a drastic step, but sometimes necessary to rectify their financial situation. This can be emotionally challenging, especially if it's the home where they raised their children and created countless memories.

However, making such difficult decisions can be a turning point. It can put them on track to achieve what most of my retired clients express as their primary goals: maintaining independence as long as possible and not becoming a burden on their children. While these decisions may not feel positive in the moment, they can lead to long-term financial security and peace of mind.

The term "Evolve" is central to my financial planning process, aptly named "The EVOLVE Advantage." This concept recognizes that change is constant in our lives. Our surroundings change, the world around us changes, and our financial situations and goals change over time. What you envision for retirement at 30 years old may be completely different from what you want at 50 years old.

The EVOLVE Advantage process is designed to deal with this constant evolution. It's not a one-time exercise but a continuous journey of adjustment and refinement. We regularly reassess situations, compare expectations with reality, and make necessary adjustments. Whether it's a pay raise, job loss, receiving an inheritance, a large liquidity event or children leaving home, these life changes require us to evolve our financial strategies.

Successful financial planning often requires an emotional attachment to your goals. If something is truly important to you, you're more likely to act and stay committed to your plan.

While the math and strategies of financial planning are important, it's often the emotional component–the commitment to a vision of your future–that drives success. By helping clients understand the truth of their situation and creating a clear, achievable plan, we can often transform fear and uncertainty into motivation and commitment.

Remember, no one's financial situation is perfect, and that's okay. The goal of this process is to design a route that works for you, considering both your current reality and your future aspirations.

To put a point on this chapter, let's talk about a client I had that had been working with me for a few years and although there was a spouse I had never met her, as my point of contact was Mr. Client. My view is that in a couple's situation we need to think of it as a team sport, and it is important that all parties are involved. However, that is not always the way it happens.

In this situation, I was meeting with Mr. Client for an annual review when he shared with me that he was dying. It didn't quite register with me what he was trying to say, and I responded to him that we all have a sale by date. That's when he shared with me that his card was going to be pulled sooner versus later. I learned that he had been in poor, declining health since the first day we met and that he was interviewing me to make sure that he had the right advisor to assist Mrs. Client after he passed away. Within about a year he did so. This is not typical, but I wanted to share this sad story as I believe that it illustrates that what we visualize the future to be is very personal. In this case, it was peace of mind in knowing that his spouse was going to be alright financially after he was gone.

CHAPTER FIVE

Orient Your Priorities:

Where Am I in Relation to My Goals?

"The worst of all deceptions is self-deception."

– Socrates

Once you have established your current financial situation and visualized your future goals, the third step in the EVOLVE Advantage process is to **Orient** yourself on the path to achieving those goals. This stage involves creating a concrete financial plan that bridges the gap between your current situation and your desired future.

The Orient step is about charting the most efficient path to your financial goals. I often use the analogy of planning a trip from Dallas to Houston. Once you know your starting point is Dallas and your destination is Houston, you can determine the most efficient route, such as Interstate 45. This becomes your roadmap.

In financial terms, this roadmap is your actual financial plan. It outlines specific actions, such as how much you need to save per paycheck, month, or year, and what financial milestones you should aim to hit at different points in time along the way.

It's important to note that this plan isn't set in stone. Your financial journey may evolve just as you might encounter detours or change destinations on a road trip. You might reach a midpoint and decide to change course entirely. The key is to reassess your position and reorient as needed periodically, it is important to remember that this is not a one and done process.

A crucial part of the orient step is discussing and understanding the pros and cons of different versions of your financial plan. We explore various paths you could take to reach your end goal. For example:

- **Retirement age scenarios:** We might compare plans for retiring at age 60, 65, or 70. Each scenario will have different savings requirements and potential lifestyle implications.
- **Education funding choices:** We could explore the financial impact of sending children to private universities versus state schools.
- **Lifestyle trade-offs:** We examine how increasing savings now might allow for earlier retirement or more financial freedom later.

We typically start with a baseline, or rough draft plan that includes straightforward needs, things that you might think of as must have goals. Then, we create different versions of the plan side by side, tweaking various factors to see their impact as we incorporate a client's vision, including not only what they consider meaningful, but the fun stuff as well. This process helps clients understand any potential trade-offs involved in different financial decisions.

Through this process, we usually converge on one version of the plan that best aligns with the client's priorities and capabilities. This might involve making sacrifices in one area to achieve goals in another. For instance, one person might be willing to save more aggressively now, while another might prefer to work longer to reach their goals.

It's important to note that these decisions don't always have to be purely logical. Sometimes, they're based on deeply held personal values or promises. Our job is to help clients understand the implications of these choices and find a balanced plan that respects their priorities while still being financially sound.

The Orient step is where the vision begins to mesh with reality, creating a concrete, actionable plan to move towards your financial goals. It's about finding the right balance between your dreams and the practical steps needed to achieve them.

During the Orient phase of financial planning, clients often experience a range of emotions. The most common is fear–fear of receiving bad news or having to make significant lifestyle changes. Many clients come in expecting to hear that their financial goals are unattainable or that they'll need to make drastic sacrifices.

This fear often stems from the vulnerability associated with discussing money. People tend to have an emotional attachment to their current lifestyle. It is not uncommon for clients to worry about potentially giving up important things like family vacations, nice cars, clothes, country club memberships or other comforts they've grown accustomed to.

Fortunately, these fears are often unfounded. In my experience, a very low percentage of clients receive truly bad news about their financial situation. Most of the time, people's financial realities are closer to what they expect, or even better. I tend to think of it as a fear of the unknown.

For older individuals or those closer to retirement, their fears often stem from knowing how difficult retirement can be. They may have watched their parents, family or friends struggle due to not being prepared and don't want to find themselves in a similar position. Also, I think that it is both strange and difficult for some people to "quit" a perfectly good job that they enjoy. However, we often find that the tough decisions and sacrifices they've made along their journey have worked to their advantage.

For younger individuals, the possibilities are often much broader, assuming a typical life span. While some may have unrealistic expectations about early retirement, their relatively young age generally provides more flexibility in planning. Essentially, they have more runway to gain the necessary speed to help the plane take off.

Of course, we have clients that are in a position where there is no doubt that they can more or less do whatever they wish, whenever they wish to do so. This is certainly an enviable position to find yourself in, but it can have its own challenges. A common concern is that their children have been fortunate enough to have been raised and to live a privileged lifestyle. And that they are potentially not very well grounded or may feel entitled. In many cases, a client may have come from a humble beginning only to become very successful financially. These clients often feel that a big reason for their success was because they had to work hard and believe in themselves. Or that they learned valuable lessons getting punched in the gut over their career.

Even when the above concerns are not an issue, wealthier clients do need to think and prepare for transitioning significant assets to their heirs in general, ensuring that their wishes are fulfilled. Also, the tax implications can be material, so having a plan in place to do so in a tax advantaged fashion needs to be a priority. Having a good estate planning attorney as part of your team is incredibly important when working through this process.

The plan that we develop isn't magical or complex and for some clients, it might simply be to continue what they're already doing. For others, it might involve some adjustments. The key is that we've agreed on a plan that's achievable and aligned with their goals.

I have a couple that I have worked with for many years. After they had been retired for ten years, their destination changed a little bit. Before retiring, they had moved around a fair amount due to the nature of the business that Mr. Client was engaged in. A town that they had lived in briefly along the way made an impression on them and that is where they decided to retire. They knew the exact area and neighborhood where they wanted to live and purchased a house that they believed would be a good fit for them. They worked hard towards getting the house and yard exactly the way they envisioned when they bought it and settled into retirement. However, after several years, it became apparent that while they loved the house, it was no longer a good fit for several reasons, one of which was accessibility due to health and mobility issues.

One idea was to simply sell their current home and find a new one that met their needs. Another option was to stay in the general area where they were, but to move to a nearby town that would get them closer to some of their family. The third idea was to return to Texas, but real estate prices had increased significantly since they had retired and especially where they had lived prior to retirement.

Eventually, they made the decision to pick up and make the move back to Texas. As part of their decision-making process, we modeled several potential options in their financial plan to rule out what wasn't financially feasible. Once we had narrowed down their options, we were able to really focus on the price range for the purchase of a new home that would allow them to continue to enjoy retirement as they had planned, but in a different location.

CHAPTER SIX

Learn Your Choices:

What Do I Need to Do?

"Tell me and I forget, teach me and I may remember, involve me and I learn."

– Benjamin Franklin

Having established your current financial situation, visualized your future goals, and oriented yourself on the path to achieve those goals, the fourth step in the EVOLVE Advantage process is the **Learn** step. This step is used to make informed financial decisions. With a vast array of financial products available, and often difficult to understand tax implications, it's essential to understand which options best align with your goals.

In this phase, we explore not only various financial products, strategies and options that could help you stay on track with your financial plan, but strategies for maximizing any benefits you have accrued from your employer or the government (example: Social Security & Medicare). We bring together ideas that we believe align with your objectives. Then, we discuss the pros and cons of each option.

It's important to note that there's no perfect solution or "silver bullet" in financial planning. Each option comes with its own set of advantages and trade-offs. Our role is to educate you on these different ideas, not to make decisions for you. We aim to be part of your team, helping you understand your options so you can choose what makes the most sense for your situation.

For instance, if you need life insurance because you have young children, we'll break down various types and familiarize you with each one. Similarly, when saving for college, we might explore options like 529 plans, Education Savings Accounts (ESAs), or taxable brokerage accounts. We'll explain why one might be more attractive than another in your specific circumstances, or why a combination might be beneficial along with the associated tax implications.

An important component of the **Learn** phase, especially if you are near or in the early stages of retirement, is how to optimize your Social Security benefit for your situation.

Social Security statistics I share with my clients to keep in mind apply to those considering claiming their benefits before Full Retirement Age (FRA). Social Security credits for each year of delayed retirement after the Normal Retirement Age (NRA) are fixed. If you were born in 1960 or later, by taking your Social Security benefit at age 62, there is a 30% discount (reduction) from your full benefit amount at your FRA. Also, it is important to understand that if you were born in 1960 or later the fixed increase once you reach your NRA for delayed retirement is 8% per year.

As you work through the process of determining when to begin taking your benefits, I feel that there are four questions that need to be thought through to do this.

1. Are you still working or not?

- How much do you make and how long do you plan to work?
- If you plan on retiring before your FRA, you must account for the penalty fees (discount/reduction).

2. How is your health?

- What can you tell me about your family history regarding longevity?
- For a healthy couple aged 65, there is a roughly 35% chance that one will live to age 95.

3. Have you ever had a spouse and if so, are they still living?

- What is the age difference?
- If there is an ex-spouse, you could be eligible for a benefit.

4. What is the current interest rate environment?

- What are they currently?

A recent development as it relates to Social Security is The Social Security Fairness Act, which was signed into law on January 5, 2025, and removes the Windfall Elimination Provision (WEP) and Government Pension Offset (GPO). These provisions previously reduced Social Security benefits for individuals who also receive pensions from jobs where they did not pay Social Security taxes, such as some public sector employees. The act ensures that these individuals receive the full Social Security benefits they are entitled to, including retroactive payments for those affected since January 1, 2024. If this applies to you then you can find more information at www.ssa.gov/benefits/retirement/social-security-fairness-act.

Many people are not aware that if you are 62 or older and have minor children (under age 18), your kids are eligible to receive a benefit based on your work history. One couple I worked with included one spouse aged 62, the other age 47 and two minor children age 3 and 5. The couple work together in a business that they own with the younger spouse being the leader of the company and the older spouse in an office manager's role.

The older spouse "retired" and began working part-time at a lower wage that would allow him to fully fund a pre-tax 401K to the maximum allowable which in 2025 would be $31,000 for anyone age 50 or more, plus a match and profit-sharing contribution, which essentially made his income $0. I do not recall the exact numbers but as an example, let's say that he started his reduced Social Security income stream of $3,000 per month in addition to his lower wage which allowed their children to receive half of his monthly benefit. However, it gets better. Each of their children will receive 50% of his benefit at full retirement age (FRA) which might have been $3,800 per month, not 50% of his reduced ($3,000 per month) benefit at age 62. The couple took the benefit for each of the children and used it to fund a 529 plan to fund college education in the future. This allowed the younger and more highly compensated spouse to let her Social Security benefit continue to grow with the plan for her not to access her benefit until age 70 when it will have maxed out.

There is a maximum family benefit so if you have lots of kids you need to be aware of and know that limit. The limit is calculated based on your benefit at FRA regardless of when you filed your benefit.

A few other important considerations are:

- When is the optimal time to start my pension income and what option should I choose?
- Are there tax strategies such as Roth conversions that I can take advantage of now or in the future to reduce taxes?
- How can I avoid or limit being forced to take income from a pre-tax retirement savings vehicle such as an IRA due to IRS rules stating that I shall take a Required Minimum Distribution (RMDs), especially if I don't need the income at that time?

Another component of the **Learn** phase is setting realistic expectations, it is important to understand the behavioral aspects of financial decision-making because emotions can play a significant role in financial choices. Just as a cookbook tells you what ingredients you need and how to put them together, we provide the information you need to understand your financial options. We explore how different choices might perform in various market conditions or scenarios. We prefer to make decisions before there is a storm, when conditions are calm. My experience has been that there is an increased risk of clients making irrational decisions in the middle of a storm. We want to avoid making long-term decisions based on short-term events.

We discuss concepts like risk tolerance and the balance between fear and greed. It's important to understand that being riskier doesn't necessarily lead to faster goal achievement; in some cases, it can be detrimental.

Every investor has a point at which losses can trigger a shift from rational to irrational decision-making. Part of our job is to help you understand your threshold for financial pain, so we can structure your investments to avoid putting you in a position where emotions or the pain of it might lead to poor choices.

In rare cases where a client insists on a course of action we strongly advise against, we may have them sign a document acknowledging our advice. This serves as a learning tool and can be instructive to review in the future.

A key part of this learning phase is understanding that market fluctuations and economic downturns are normal and somewhat predictable surprises, meaning that we don't know when they will happen, but we do know that we will have down markets on occasion. We educate clients about the normalcy of economic cycles, including recessions and market corrections. By setting proper expectations upfront, we aim to make it easier for clients to handle market volatility when it occurs, thereby increasing their probability of long-term success.

This step is more than just understanding financial products. It's about gaining insights into your financial behavior, setting realistic expectations, and preparing for the inevitable ups and downs of the financial markets. This knowledge forms the foundation for making sound financial decisions aligned with your long-term goals. We encourage our clients to approach these events with an open mind, understanding which areas of their financial plan carry more risk and what kinds of surprises they might encounter.

Developing intentional self-awareness about how you respond when things aren't going perfectly in the market is vital. Some key points to consider:

- Identify your threshold for financial pain: the point at which you might shift from rational to irrational decision-making.
- Understand your emotional responses to market ups and downs.
- Recognize that it's normal to feel emotional about your money–you've worked hard for it.

We emphasize focusing on what you can control in your financial life:

- How long you work
- How much do you save
- How much you spend
- How much risk do you take

Everyone has a unique financial personality, often influenced by their experiences, upbringing, and natural tendencies. In couples, we often see contrasting approaches to money management:

- An aggressive investor paired with a more conservative one
- A "money person" partnered with someone less interested in finances
- A worrier matched with a more carefree individual

Understanding these dynamics helps when working with couples. Remember, it is a team sport. Our goal is to find a compromise that both parties are comfortable with. Concentrating on these aspects can help you better navigate the uncontrollable elements of the financial markets.

Additionally, constantly checking your account balances can lead to emotional decision-making. For example, you might feel like you've lost money if you invested $500,000 that grew to $1 million and then pulled back to $800,000 during a market downturn. You may feel that you have lost money , but in reality, you've still gained $300,000 on your initial investment. This kind of thinking can lead to poor financial choices driven by emotion rather than logic.

These concepts often need consistent reinforcement. Even if a client doesn't fully internalize this information initially, having heard it before can be helpful when facing a real financial challenge. It's about planting seeds that may sprout and become useful during tough times.

That being said, there's no universally right or wrong approach to finances. A significant part of our job is helping you figure out who you are financially. This self-discovery process is especially important for those new to the concept of financial planning.

Again, it's normal to feel emotional about your money–the key is to balance those emotions with rational decision-making based on your long-term financial plan. By understanding your financial personality, preparing for market fluctuations, focusing on what you can control, and developing self-awareness about your emotional responses to financial events, you can make more informed decisions and stay the course during challenging times.

To conclude this chapter, I will tell you about one of our services that had a big impact on a client but let's start with raising your hand if you enjoy paying taxes…well, not everyone at once! I have yet to meet the person who enjoys paying taxes and I include myself. Taxes are a necessary evil, and I must admit that I like driving on paved roads, having water come out when I turn on the faucet and the idea that there are firemen and police officers around the corner to help me if needed. That said, we work with our clients to reduce their tax outlay as much as possible within the IRS rules.

One of the ways that we benefit our clients is through the Learning phase of our process. The better we get to know our clients, their situation and their future plans, the better we are positioned to help them. We can teach and educate them on ideas that we believe might be useful and at times, we bring strategies that they did not know existed.

A business owner client that we work with is a great example of this in real life. Mr. and Mrs. Client were nearing retirement and although they had scaled back their business significantly, things were going very well, and they knew that the last two to three years before retiring and closing their business they were going to make a good chunk of money in a short period of time. The problem was that there was going to be a significant tax event coming fairly soon.

As part of the learning that we brought to the table, we educated them on the concept of using a defined benefit pension plan to limit and defer some of their tax outlay. There was north of $1,000,000 that would be paid out to them as W2 income and taxed at roughly 40%. Due to the reduced size of the business (less employees), they were able to start a defined benefit plan and include the husband, wife and one employee in the plan based on the rules and guidelines that govern this type of plan. They had the flexibility to split most of the fees that they were receiving from their client over two years; a portion in the fall and the remainder the next spring. That allowed them to split the actual amount that they were taking as taxable income over two tax years, which is simple enough.

However, using the defined benefit plan they were able to drop roughly $400,000 into a tax-deductible, tax-deferred account for their benefit. Their employee contribution was roughly 4%, so around $16,000 with the remaining $384,000 going to the two of them. I do want to note that they will pay taxes when they eventually make a distribution from their pre-tax IRAs, which is where the balances were eventually parked once they were retired, but we expected that they would be in a lower tax bracket once they were retired. But 40% of $400,000 is a tax savings of $160,000 of which 96% went to the husband/wife business owners. This strategy doesn't work for every or even most situations, but when it fits it can be very attractive.

I want to remind you that I have yet to retire myself, but I have had the opportunity to retire multiple times over the years with my clients. In doing so, I have valuable experience that I can share. The goal is to help you make informed decisions.

CHAPTER SEVEN

Vote Your Decision:

Make a Decision and Take Action

"Never mistake motion for action."

– Ernest Hemingway

Building upon all the previous steps in which you have established your current financial situation, visualized your future goals, oriented yourself on the path to achieving those goals, and learned to make informed financial decisions, the fifth step in the EVOLVE Advantage process is **Vote.** The "Vote" step is where the rubber meets the road. Until this point, clients have invested time and effort in understanding their financial situation, exploring options, and learning about strategies that fit their situations. Now, it's time to make decisions and act.

Without action, your financial situation will not change. Voting is the second most important piece of the process, right after the initial "Establish" step. While establishing your financial situation creates momentum, voting is where you commit to the path forward.

When working with a financial advisor, the Vote process involves two key decisions:

1. **Choosing your financial advisor:** Deciding if we're a good fit and if you want us to be your financial guide.

2. **Committing to action:** Agreeing to take the necessary steps to work towards the goals and dreams we've established in the previous steps.

This is the point where you're ready to act because you know how the plan solves a problem or creates an opportunity for you. It's like jumping into the deep end of the pool–you're fully committing to your financial journey.

The Vote step involves practical actions such as:

- Signing paperwork
- Opening accounts
- Funding investments
- Purchasing insurance if needed
- Connecting with other professionals (e.g., attorneys for Wills, CPAs for additional tax advice) as needed

For many clients, this step brings a sense of accomplishment and relief. It's the moment you can exhale, knowing you've taken a significant step towards your financial goals.

The emotions at this stage are often a mix of excitement and apprehension:

- **Excitement:** If we've done our job well in communicating clearly and effectively, and have truly understood your goals, you should feel excited about moving forward. It's like the moment you board a plane for a planned vacation–it's no longer just talk, it's real and happening.

- **Apprehension:** Some nervousness is normal, especially for less experienced investors or those who tend to worry. The unknown always carries some level of anxiety.

On our end, when our clients decide and **Vote**, we do the heavy lifting. We spring into action and create the necessary accounts, fill out any needed applications, and fund the mapped-out investments.

One particular situation stands out as it relates to the Vote phase. Anyone who has watched a family member or friend go through the aging process knows that it can be difficult to watch and experience. Some of us will do better than others, but unfortunately, it is common for our bodies and minds to not cooperate over time. Often it can be managed by loved ones simply checking in on mom or dad, but in other scenarios that is just not enough. Maybe you need to have someone spend 2 or 3 days a week onsite or possibly an assisted living arrangement where a loved one has a tremendous amount of independence. Many times, what started as a limited amount of care oftentimes increases to what I would call acute care such as a memory unit or more traditional nursing home care. Not only is seeing a loved one in this scenario difficult to watch and deal with emotionally, but it is expensive. In a couple's situation this can get tricky and has the potential to derail continuing to have the independence that most of us would like to experience.

A common risk that I share and work with my clients to resolve is a situation where one of them needs care sooner rather than later, but the other spouse continues to be in good health and have a much longer life expectancy. If one spouse needed expensive care early in retirement and for several years, the cost could be incredibly expensive. Many of you have experienced this firsthand, others have heard stories and watched from afar. If you have done so, you understand how expensive care can be.

Let's be honest, we all know that you would do whatever it takes at whatever cost you can bear to take care of someone important to you. The potential issue is that it is quite possible that you end up with expenses as if you were running two households: the cost of care for a loved one and the cost of maintaining a home and life for the healthier spouse. The reality is that most of us cannot do this for very long, if at all, without significantly spending down our retirement assets or depleting them entirely. Should this happen, you could find yourself losing much of your independence along with the feeling that you are being a burden on your children.

The good news is that there is a simple, straight forward way to deal with this risk head-on, long term care insurance. Long term care insurance comes in primarily two different flavors and several variations that are too detailed to share here. The important thing to understand is that by using a one-time lump sum or monthly premium payment you can get insurance coverage that depending on how you structure it, you can access to cover all or a portion of any potential expense related to long term care.

Several years ago, I had a couple that was nearing retirement and when someone is at that stage in life, we discuss the possibility that one or both could need long term care in the future and that it is not inexpensive. We reviewed strategies that might make sense to plan for this potential eventuality including the purchase of long-term care insurance. Ultimately, they made the decision to get coverage on each of them. Unfortunately, in about 6 – 7 years Mr. Client began showing signs of dementia. Mrs. Client and some family that lived nearby were able to provide a level of care that was adequate for a year or so, but eventually Mr. Client needed to be at a facility and within maybe another year or two he was in a memory unit. All told, he was in care for roughly 4 years before passing away.

Thankfully, they had decided to Vote and make the decision to purchase long-term care insurance coverage that covered essentially 100% of his very expensive care. That was 9 years ago now and Mrs. Client remains healthy, active and financially sound. By making the decision to act and not kick the can down the road, she was able to make a difficult situation a little bit easier and less scary.

With the **Vote** step completed, we're ready to implement your financial plan. Your financial journey is ongoing, but you've committed to a clear path forward with this step. You're now actively working towards your financial goals and dreams. While there's one more step in the EVOLVE Advantage process, this is the point where many clients feel they've truly accomplished something significant.

CHAPTER EIGHT

Evaluate Your Success:

Are You Making Progress?

"Success is not the final; failure is not fatal. It is the courage to continue that counts."

– Winston Churchill

The final step in the EVOLVE Advantage process is to **Evaluate**, which comes after you have established your current financial situation, visualized your future goals, oriented yourself on the path to achieving those goals, learned to make informed financial decisions, and voted to commit to the path forward. The "Evaluate" step is a crucial component, focusing on ongoing assessment and adjustment of your financial plan. This step ensures that your financial strategy remains aligned with your goals and adapts to life changes.

We implement a system of regular check-ups, similar to annual medical or dental check-ups. Each client is assigned an annual review month when we proactively reach out to schedule a time to meet and review any changes to their situation and update their financial plan as needed. These reviews are essential for several reasons:

- To identify any changes in the client's life or goals
- To evaluate your progress as it relates to your financial plan

- To make necessary adjustments to the strategy
- To ensure clients understand and are satisfied with our services

I often draw parallels between financial planning and dental hygiene. Just as you brush your teeth daily and visit the dentist regularly to prevent long-term problems, consistent attention to your finances is equally important. If you neglect your teeth today there generally will not be any consequences; however, if you neglect them for 30 years, they will more than likely fall out. Similarly, if you neglect your finances for 30 years, you'll face the financial equivalent of your teeth falling out–a retirement without adequate resources.

During the evaluation process, we revisit the financial plan to compare projected outcomes with actual results. We assess whether we are making progress per the original plan's parameters, and how we define success. This involves:

1. Reviewing the original goals and projections
2. Analyzing the actual outcome to date
3. Identifying any discrepancies or unexpected results
4. Determining if adjustments are needed

Life is dynamic, and your financial plan should be too. Even if you don't actively make changes, certain milestones can impact your financial situation:

- Career changes or pay raises
- Children moving out of the house

- Aging into new financial stages (e.g., becoming eligible for penalty-free retirement account withdrawals at 59½)
- Relocation plans, perhaps to be closer to grandchildren
- Qualifying for Medicare at 65
- Health events, both large and small

We use the evaluation process to identify these changes and adjust your financial strategy accordingly.

One of the most important financial transitions to understand is the shift from the accumulation phase to the distribution phase. Just as "sports" is an overarching term used to describe distinct categories like baseball and football, finance is the same way. Finance is an overarching term that also consists of different phases with unique characteristics. The first phase–what we have talked about for most of this book–is the accumulation phase, where you are focusing on building your net worth and following your plan as you prepare for retirement.

Then, as you transition into retirement and begin to live off your savings, you enter the distribution phase. Much like how baseball and football are completely different sports with their own rules and strategies, accumulation and distribution are separate financial phases requiring different skills. As mentioned in an earlier chapter, having a sherpa guiding you on your financial journey is extremely helpful. Not only do they lead you on your journey and help you avoid pitfalls along the way, but they also help guide you back down the mountain to safety. I like to think of accumulation as climbing Mt Everest and distribution as descending. Not being able to navigate each of these phases could end in catastrophe. Interestingly, the majority of climbers on Mt Everest perished on the trip down the mountain.

Another practice I stand by is face-to-face meetings for annual reviews whenever it is possible to do so. While technology allows for remote communications, these in-person interactions often lead to better conversations and allow us to catch up on important life events that might not seem financial at first glance but could have an impact on your overall strategy.

Face-to-face meetings also help us uncover information that clients might not think to share proactively. You might not think of calling us immediately when you change jobs, remodel your home, buy a new vehicle, or when your child chooses a college, but these events can impact your financial plan.

Our expectation is that we will have a review annually; however, the frequency of full plan reviews can vary:

- For clients within five to ten years of retirement or a major financial goal, we typically review the comprehensive plan annually.
- For clients further from major milestones, we might conduct full plan reviews every other year, assuming no significant life changes.

The evaluation process requires active client participation. While some individuals might not see the value in annual reviews if they perceive no major changes, it's crucial to understand that small changes can accumulate over time and impact your financial trajectory.

We encourage all clients to participate in these annual reviews. Your engagement in the process is vital for maintaining sound financial hygiene and achieving optimal long-term outcomes. I often tell clients, "I don't think it's a good thing if I'm taking your financial situation more to heart than you are."

The Evaluate step ensures that your financial plan evolves with you, adapting to changes in your life and the broader economic environment. By regularly assessing and adjusting your strategy, we can help increase your odds of achieving your financial goals. This step embodies the "Evolve" in our EVOLVE Advantage process. Things are constantly changing; at a minimum, you're a year older with each review. We need to assess how these changes, whether minor or significant, impact your financial plan.

One of my more memorable client experiences that fall under the Evaluate step involved clients taking a substantial tax hit “today” in order to benefit from the “lifetime of taxes” concept. I work with a couple who are outstanding savers, and we had assisted them in consolidating several old 401K plans and other assorted IRA’s with a combined balance of $300,000 to $400,000 or so. During our annual reviews with clients, we typically touch on taxes as it is a standard agenda item. I don’t recall what exactly got us going down the road of converting 100% of their IRA’s to a Roth IRA, which is a taxable event in general and a significant outlay on such a large amount, but we did.

They had a good amount in a taxable account that was available to use to cover the tax hit if they were to convert all the IRAs at once. Not only were they great about saving, but they were also relatively young, I would say approximately 35 years old at the time. Converting an IRA to a Roth means that you pay taxes in the year you convert it at ordinary income tax rates. Such a large amount along with their earned income would push them into the top tax bracket. Once you get past the tax hit in the year that you convert, the balance will grow tax-deferred and come out tax free at their retirement. Another benefit of a Roth IRA is that you are not forced to take a Required Minimum Distribution (RMD) once you are in your 70's, which you would have to do with a traditional IRA. I think of RMD's as the government wanting to get Uncle Sam's return on your investment.

In a situation like this, the math is simple, and it helped that they had a long runway due to their age. If the amount of growth over time exceeds and then some, the amount paid in tax to convert it now makes financial sense. Remember, that 100% of distributions from a Roth IRA, including the growth, are distributed tax-free. Math is one thing, and yes, it informed us that converting is a smart financial decision given their situation but being on the hook for an additional tax of roughly $150,000 or so is a different emotion. Ultimately, they made the difficult, but prudent decision to convert all their IRA money to Roth IRAs. It is difficult for me to know the actual amount from their prior conversions now in their Roth IRAs as we have folded other retirement plans into those accounts, but I feel comfortable that they have covered the amount of the tax hit by two times, if not three times at this point.

CONCLUSION

The Outcome You Deserve

"The only place success comes before work is in the dictionary."

– Vince Lombardi

It's important to recognize that the path to financial well-being is not a finite journey with a fixed endpoint. Rather, it's an ongoing process of evaluation, adjustment, and growth. The promised land of financial security isn't a distant, unreachable dream. It's a reality that can be achieved through consistent effort, informed decision-making, and a commitment to your financial health.

While some individuals may have the expertise and inclination to manage their finances independently, many benefit from professional guidance. Finding a financial advisor who aligns with your values and communication style can be invaluable in navigating the complexities of financial and tax planning. Remember the young nurse we discussed earlier? Her success story exemplifies the power of consistent saving and good financial habits, guided by professional advice. This achievement wasn't due to extraordinary income or investment picks, but rather the result of consistent, early, and frequent saving, coupled with the discipline to let the money grow undisturbed.

One of the key messages of the EVOLVE Advantage is the importance of getting started. The sooner you begin your financial planning journey, the more time to benefit from the process.

Whether you're in your 20s just starting your career, in your 50s looking towards retirement, or currently retired The EVOLVE Advantage process can help you **Establish** where you are, **Visualize** where you want to go, **Orient** yourself on the right path, **Learn** about your options, **Vote** on the path forward, and continually **Evaluate** and adjust your plan.

The ultimate destination in financial planning isn't a specific number in your bank account or a particular net worth. Instead, it's a state of mind and a set of circumstances:

- **Peace of Mind:** Achieving a level of financial security that allows you to live without constant worry about money.
- **Protection for Loved Ones:** Ensuring that those around you are taken care of, regardless of what might happen.
- **Preparedness:** Being ready for both the expected milestones and unexpected challenges life may bring.
- **Freedom to Enjoy Life:** Having the resources to pursue your dreams, whether that's traveling, spending time with family, or pursuing hobbies.
- **Setting a Positive Example:** Demonstrating good financial habits that can inspire others, particularly younger generations, to make sound financial decisions.

Going through the process to develop a financial plan is not a one-time event but a continuous process. Life unfolds, goals change, and economic conditions fluctuate. The Evolve Advantage process is designed to adapt to changes, constantly re-evaluate, and adjust your financial strategy.

In essence, the EVOLVE Advantage process is about empowering you to take control of your financial future. It's about making informed decisions, avoiding common pitfalls, and working consistently towards your goals. By following this process and working with a trusted advisor, you can create a financial foundation that supports your life goals and provides security for you and your loved ones. The peace of mind that comes from knowing you're financially prepared can significantly enhance your quality of life, allowing you to focus on living and enjoying life rather than constantly worrying about financial matters. I believe that with the right relationships, we can build anything that we set in our mind to do.

The journey to financial well-being is ongoing. It requires consistent attention and adjustment, but the rewards—peace of mind, security, and the freedom to live life on your terms—are well worth the effort.

You're not alone. It's not easy. But you'll eventually get there if you keep focusing and working toward your goals. Maybe not in the way you originally envisioned. There will be bumps in the road—unexpected challenges, detours, and moments of doubt. I know this because I've been there myself. I've seen my clients face these same obstacles, and I've helped them navigate through them.

That's why I developed the EVOLVE Advantage system, because we are always evolving. Where I was five, ten, twenty, even thirty years ago is a far cry from where I am today. My priorities, my strategies, and my understanding of the financial world have all changed. And that's the point. You must keep paying attention:

- Where am I now?
- Where do I want to go?
- What did I think would happen?
- What actually happened?
- What adjustments do I need to make?

Some parts of my journey turned out as expected, but many did not. That's life. The key is to stay flexible, keep learning, and be willing to adjust.

The purpose of this book is to give you a framework, a way to approach your financial life with clarity, whether you choose to navigate it on your own or with the help of a trusted advisor. My hope is that it makes your path a little easier and that it reassures you that even for someone like me, a financial advisor, the road is rarely a straight line.

The struggles you're facing. They're normal. The frustration? It's expected. No, it's not fun when you're in the thick of it. But don't let the tough times weigh you down. Just keep putting one foot in front of the other. Progress happens in small steps. How do you eat an elephant? One bite at a time.

Find someone to share your journey with, whether it's a spouse, a family member, or a trusted financial advisor. Having a sounding board, a voice of reason, can make all the difference. It can help steady you when emotions run high and keep you focused on what really matters.

I've walked this path. I've helped others walk it. And I believe that if you stay committed, keep learning, and remain adaptable, you'll find your own version of success, whatever that may look like for you.

Disclosures

Not an Offer, Recommendation or Professional Advice

The information provided and the views expressed herein do not constitute a recommendation or investment advice of any kind nor are they an offer or solicitation to buy or sell any securities or to adopt any investment strategies or financial products. This material is not intended to be relied upon as a forecast or research in any way and should not be solely relied upon when making an investment decision. This material is provided solely for informational purposes and on the understanding that the recipient has sufficient knowledge and experience to be able to understand and make their own evaluations of the proposals and services described herein, any risks associated therewith, and any related legal, tax, accounting, or other material considerations. To the extent that the reader has any questions about the applicability of any specific issue discussed above to their specific portfolio or situation, they are encouraged to contact or consult with the professional advisor of their choosing. Opinions and commentary do not take into account the investment objectives or financial situation of any particular investor or class of investors. Investors will need to consider their own circumstances before making an investment decision. Investment allocations are subject to change and should not be construed as investment advice. Except where otherwise indicated, the information contained herein is based on matters as they exist as of the date of preparation of such material and not as of the date of distribution or any future date. Recipients should not rely on this material in making any future investment decision.

Use of Third-Party Information

Certain information contained herein has been obtained from third party sources and such information has not been independently verified by SageSpring Wealth Partners LLC ("SageSpring"). No representation, warranty, or undertaking, expressed or implied, is given to the accuracy or completeness of such information by SageSpring or any other person. While such sources are believed to be reliable, SageSpring does not assume any responsibility for the accuracy or completeness of such information. SageSpring does not undertake any obligation to update the information contained herein as of any future date.

Past Performance

All investments involve risk, including possible loss of principal. There is no guarantee that the investment objectives will be achieved. Moreover, the past performance is not a guarantee or indicator of future results, which may vary. Except where otherwise indicated, the information contained in this presentation is based on matters as they exist as of the date of preparation of such material and not as of the date of distribution or any future date.

Views and Opinions

The views and opinions expressed herein are for educational purposes only and do not represent any recommendations to invest by SageSpring.

Made in the USA
Coppell, TX
07 June 2026

78435800R00046